DOMESTIC VIOLENCE
Assault on a Woman's Worth

JUNE HUNT

ROSE PUBLISHING/ASPIRE PRESS

Peabody, Massachusetts

ROSE PUBLISHING/ASPIRE PRESS

Domestic Violence: Assault on a Woman's Worth
Copyright © 2013 Hope For The Heart
All rights reserved.
Aspire Press, an imprint of Hendrickson Publishers Marketing, LLC
P.O. Box 3473
Peabody, Massachusetts 01961-3473 USA

www.HendricksonRose.com

Register your book at www.aspirepress.com/register
Get inspiration via email, sign up at www.aspirepress.com

Printed in the United States of America
040617VP

CONTENTS

Definitions..8

What Is Abuse?....................................9

What Are the Different Types of Abuse?.............12

Where Is God in All of This?....................21

Characteristics...................................26

What Is the Cycle of Abuse?....................27

What Is the Situational Setup for Abuse?.............30

What Is the Cost of Being
  Constantly Abused?............................33

What Choices Can Be Considered?.....................35

Causes...38

Why Does He Do It?...............................39

Why Doesn't She Leave?..........................41

Why Does She Leave?.............................45

Why Does She Feel Guilty?.......................49

Root Cause..53

How to Seek Significance
  and Find Security in God.....................56

Steps to Solution.................................60

How to Correct the Confusion...................61

How to Know Whether He Has
  Really Changed.................................66

How to Build Healthy Boundaries.................68

How to Prepare a Safety Plan...................75

How to Protect Yourself Outside the Home.........81

How to Use the Law in the U.S. 83

How to Realize Your Biblical Bill of Rights.........89

ear friend,

"Intelligent, competent, assured"

These words painted the picture of an attractive, energetic young woman whom I had known casually for over ten years. But when I received word that, at the hands of her husband, she had been a victim of repeated violence, my first thought was, *How could this be?*

After all, she had worked for several years at a Christian ministry training people how to study the Bible. Then she attended a respected seminary where she met her future husband. However, after they married, her confidence decreased and her fear increased. Unbeknownst to family and friends, she was being abused.

How could she tell anyone? She wanted to protect the image of her little family. Surely if she "tried hard enough" he would stop; typically that's what all abused women think. But not so. Now he was divorcing her for another woman, and they were in the midst of a custody battle over their two young sons.

The judge ruled that until a decision was made as to which parent would have custodial care, this arrangement was to be followed: The children were to stay in the home, and each parent would rotate in and out every other week. So every other week for about a year and a half, she stayed in my home.

We had many late night talks. The one that stands out most in my memory was the evening I asked if she had any pictures to prove to the judge that her husband was an untrustworthy, violent man. Immediately she went to the guest bedroom and returned with pictures of herself—police photographs that showed her head severely bruised and swollen. I was stunned. I hadn't expected such graphic pictures. (Her husband had denied the abuse, claiming instead that she had inflicted the injuries on herself—a common "blame game" tactic!)

When I gave her this material on domestic violence, she quickly identified with the "Scripture twisting." This simply means that many wife batterers are adept at manipulating their wives with Scriptures, such as Ephesians 5:22—*"Wives, submit to your husbands"*—but are careless about heeding all the verses against violence. (And sadly, as of yet, I have never talked with an abused woman who has heard Scriptures presented from the pulpit that encourage her to seek the protection she so desperately needs.)

Rather, after an incident of abuse, too many women hear foolish statements like, *What did you do to cause it?* This indicates that his violent sin is her fault. (Now she is being doubly victimized.)

It is no surprise that many women who suffer abuse are disheartened, confused and distressed. They wonder, *Must I really suffer at the hands of someone who has sworn to protect and cherish me? And where is God when I am hurting so much?*

The greater truth is that God is not only with those who suffer, but that He also has provided a way of deliverance through His Word. The joy of victory and healing is available to any who seek it. My prayer is that the biblical truths shared within the pages of this book will be used by God to free you or someone you know from the shackles of unjust suffering.

Yours in the Lord's hope,

June

June Hunt

P.S. Now, for the rest of the story: First, after two years, my friend was awarded custody of her children. Second, the judge admitted that, in retrospect, his better judgment would have been to assign only one parent custodial care until a permanent decision was made. And last, my friend's ex-husband served no time in jail and received no sentencing for his abuse.

"Do not make friends with a hot-tempered man,
do not associate with one easily angered."
(Proverbs 22:24)

DOMESTIC VIOLENCE
Assault on a Woman's Worth

This story is real. The facts are true.

He is prominent and highly esteemed, praised for his significant contributions to the community. What woman wouldn't feel fortunate to be his wife? She certainly has all the finer things in life. And the children have the best that money can buy. How could she think of destroying such a picture-perfect family? How could she risk losing her security or stepping into an unknown future?

Where would she go? What could she do? How would she support herself? Even worse, if she began to expose the terrible truth, would she lose her children?

She feels hopeless. Who would believe her? No one could conceive that such a pillar of the community could pummel his wife night after night with painful punches. She is skilled at hiding her feelings, as well as her bruises. With swollen, tear-stained eyes, she wrongfully reasons, *It's mostly my fault anyway!*

But her Creator God knows the undeniable truth:

"You hear, O Lord, the desire of the afflicted; you encourage them, and you listen to their cry, defending the fatherless and the oppressed, in order that man, who is of the earth, may terrify no more."
(Psalm 10:17–18)

DEFINITIONS

God designed the marriage relationship to balance, to benefit, and to better one another. With the first marriage on earth, He created Eve to be the perfect companion for Adam. He intended the pair to love, honor, and cherish each other all the days of their lives, just as He intends for every married couple today.

But in too many homes around the world, the marriage bond has become bondage—shared lives have become shattered by abuse. Husbands are berating, belittling, betraying their wives. Yet these secret assaults stay hidden from the outside world. The sacred relationship created by God has been undermined by one mate hurting—even harming—the other.

Any form of abuse is a flagrant violation of the marriage vows, "To have and to hold from this day forward ... to love and to cherish, 'til death do us part." And although such abuse is too frequently "behind closed doors," it is blatantly in open view before the eyes of the Lord.

**"Nothing in all creation
is hidden from God's sight.
Everything is uncovered and laid bare
before the eyes of him to whom
we must give account."
(Hebrews 4:13)**

While abusive acts are committed by both men and women, in cases of domestic violence approximately 95% of victims are women.[1] Although abusive treatment has a long history of being tolerated socially and even legally, abuse has always grieved the heart of God.

In certain countries, wife beating is considered a cultural norm. The majority of health-care workers in those countries, both male and female, condone husbands using physical force against their wives under certain circumstances, resulting in abused women who are receiving little or no emotional support from the national health-care system. For example, if a Turkish wife criticizes her husband, the public supports his inflicting her with painful blows as her rightful punishment.[2]

Often, women suffering in other countries get little help from those around them, but help is available from Someone above them. God promises to be close to the brokenhearted, to compassionately care, and to comfort the abused.

> **"He heals the brokenhearted
> and binds up their wounds."
> (Psalm 147:3)**

▶ **Abuse** means "to mistreat, hurt, or injure."[3]

▶ **Abuse** and **violence** are often used interchangeably, although the word *violence* implies an escalation of abuse and introduces the element of fear of harm as a means of control.[4]

▶ **Violence**, in Hebrew, is most often a translation of the word *chamas*, which means "to wrong" or "treat violently."[5] *Chamas* is also translated as "malicious, destroy, wrong, crime, ruthless, plunder," and "terror."[6]

God feels the strongest opposition against anyone who is abusive or violent toward another.

> **"'I hate a man's covering himself with violence ...' says the LORD Almighty."**
> **(Malachi 2:16)**

▶ **Domestic violence** and **family violence** are the legal terms for physical spousal abuse, child abuse, elder abuse, or any other physically abusive relationship within the home or family.[7]

▶ **Domestic violence refers to a pattern** of coercive and violent behaviors exercised by one adult in an intimate relationship with another.[8]

▶ **Domestic violence is *not*** an issue of "marriage problems" or "irreconcilable differences" solved by "conflict resolution." This kind of abuse ...

A—**Affects everyone in the family**

B—**Bridges all levels in society: racial, religious, geographic, and economic**

U—**Undermines the value of others**

S—**Seeks to dominate others**

E—**Escalates in intensity and frequency**

Spiritual leaders, community officials, family, and friends need to be responsive when informed of domestic violence. Abuse of any kind should never be tolerated nor hidden under the cover of male supremacy or "godly submission." To the contrary, the God of the Bible is our God of refuge—a stronghold of support and defense against violence.

We are to call upon Him:

"My rock, in whom I take refuge, my shield and the horn of my salvation.
He is my stronghold, my refuge and my savior—from violent men you save me."
(2 Samuel 22:3)

Abuse and Punishment for Sins

QUESTION: **"Would God condone my mate abusing me in order to punish me for my sins?"**

ANSWER: No. Many instances in Scripture show where God used one nation to bring judgment on another nation. However, there is no instance where God used the violence of one mate to punish the other mate. God hates sin, and abuse is sin. The truth is:

- An abusive mate is abusive simply as a result of choosing wrong over right.

- While you may be the recipient of abuse, you are not the *reason* for that abuse.

- Your mate's violence exposes his sinfulness, not your sinfulness.

God's instruction for all of us is to ...

**"Do what is just and right. ...
Do no wrong or violence."
(Jeremiah 22:3)**

WHAT ARE the Different Types of Abuse?[9]

Do you think you can always identify abuse when it is happening? The truth is, probably not. Abusive behavior can be aggressive or passive, physical or psychological, direct or indirect. Regardless of the method, all abusive behavior comes from those with hardened hearts who want to punish, coerce, and control.

Although abusers treat their mates unjustly, they blame their mates for their abusive actions: "You made me do it!" "If it weren't for you I would never have done it!" It is never the abusive man's fault—or so he hurtfully says.

After the pileup of put-downs, harsh beatings, and even sadistic sexual acts, women can tragically start to believe, *He's probably right.* It really is all my fault. But God knows the abusive man is entirely wrong. And He knows precisely what is in the abuser's heart: Along with deception resides another evil—injustice.

**"In your heart you devise injustice,
and your hands mete out
violence on the earth."
(Psalm 58:2)**

Verbal Abuse

Verbal abuse is the use of words or tone of voice in an attempt to control, hurt another person, or to destroy that person's self-worth. Like physical abuse, verbal abuse is devastating within a relationship—a destroyer of respect, trust, and intimacy.

Place a check mark (✔) beside any of the following behaviors that you have used or that have been used against you.

▶ **Verbally abusive language** is characterized by:

- ☐ *Badgering* with excessive questioning or accusations
- ☐ *Belittling* by mocking or name-calling
- ☐ *Blaming* you for the abuse
- ☐ *Confusing* with mind games or twisting what is said
- ☐ *Controlling* with criticism or sarcasm
- ☐ *Degrading* with public or private put-downs
- ☐ *Demoralizing* by making light of the abusive behavior
- ☐ *Devaluing* by demeaning family or friends
- ☐ *Disempowering* by continually dictating orders
- ☐ *Disrespecting* by denying that the abuse ever happened
- ☐ *Insulting* with coarse language or profanity
- ☐ *Intimidating* with yelling or threats
- ☐ *Manipulating* with threats of self-injury or suicide

- ☐ *Overpowering* by always claiming to be right
- ☐ *Paralyzing* by threatening to report you as an unfit parent
- ☐ *Shaming* with humiliation or "guilt trips"
- ☐ *Silencing* with constant interruptions or by changing topics
- ☐ *Telling* half-truths or lies

The internal negative impact of verbal abuse can last much longer than the external negative impact of physical violence. Name-calling, derogatory comments, persistent shaming, ridicule, and threats are devastating and highly destructive, making the victim (whether man or woman) even more vulnerable to being controlled by the abuser.

The psalmist says of the verbal abuser:

> **"His mouth is full of curses and lies**
> **and threats; trouble and evil**
> **are under his tongue."**
> **(Psalm 10:7)**

Emotional Abuse

While all forms of mistreatment are emotionally abusive, certain overt behaviors can be labeled as **emotional abuse**. All acts of emotional abuse will fit into one of two categories: passive or aggressive.

Place a check mark (✔) beside any of the following behaviors that have been used against you.

▶ **Passive emotional abuse** is characterized by:

☐ *Avoiding* the giving of deserved compliments to you

☐ *Brooding* and sulking when around you

☐ *Changing* your passwords linked to financial accounts

☐ *Denying* your request to leave when you ask

☐ *Displaying* continual irritability around you

☐ *Disrespecting* your rights, opinions, or feelings

☐ *Failing* to return to your home at a reasonable time

☐ *Forbidding* access to your money, checkbook, and/or credit cards

☐ *Holding* back appropriate attention from you

☐ *Keeping* you from getting help to overcome an addiction

☐ *Manipulating* your children

☐ *Monitoring* all of your computer usage

☐ *Neglecting* your important family gatherings

☐ *Refusing* to express true feelings with you

☐ *Rejecting* your need for emotional support

☐ *Resisting* helping you with the children

☐ *Stopping* important information from getting to you

☐ *Being unwilling* to take a fair share of responsibility with you

☐ *Using* the "silent treatment" against you

☐ *Withholding* a listening ear from you or a response requested by you

The psalmist describes the feelings of the person who is being emotionally abused:

> "My soul is in anguish. ...
> I am ... utterly crushed;
> I groan in anguish of heart."
> (Psalm 6:3; 38:8)

▶ **Aggressive emotional abuse** is characterized by:

- ☐ *Blocking* the doorway when you are arguing
- ☐ *Breaking* promises to you or not keeping agreements
- ☐ *Checking* up on you continually
- ☐ *Damaging* your treasured items
- ☐ *Demanding* that you behave adoringly in public after abusing you
- ☐ *Driving* recklessly to instill fear in you
- ☐ *Expressing* excessive anger toward you
- ☐ *Forbidding* you from seeking necessary medical treatment
- ☐ *Harassing* you with unwanted phone calls
- ☐ *Hiding* your car keys as a means of control
- ☐ *Interfering* with your work
- ☐ *Interrupting* your sleep
- ☐ *Intimidating* you with threatening gestures or body language
- ☐ *Isolating* you from family and friends
- ☐ *Making* unwanted visits to you
- ☐ *Manipulating* your decision making
- ☐ *Monitoring* all of your phone calls

- ☐ *Prohibiting* your participation in major decisions
- ☐ *Stalking* you
- ☐ *Suspecting* your activities with excessive jealousy
- ☐ *Threatening* you with weapons

The psalmist describes the aggressive emotional abuser:

> **"In his arrogance the wicked man hunts down the weak, who are caught in the schemes he devises."**
> **(Psalm 10:2)**

Physical Abuse/Violence

Physical abuse involves a person's use of physical size, strength, presence, or position to control or hurt someone else. Often beginning with verbal threats of physical harm—"You'll wish you had never been born!"—the verbal abuse escalates to physical abuse; the threats become reality.

The first act of violence makes it easier for the abuser to be violent again if there are no immediate repercussions. Once the taboo is broken—"never hit a woman"—minor attacks can escalate into major assaults.

Place a check mark (✓) beside any of the following behaviors that you have committed or that you have received.

▶ **Acts of violence** include:

☐ Pushing/shoving	☐ Hitting walls
☐ Slapping/striking	☐ Shaking severely
☐ Kicking/stomping	☐ Slamming doors
☐ Grabbing/choking	☐ Throwing objects
☐ Burning/scalding	☐ Breaking teeth
☐ Binding/chaining	☐ Breaking items
☐ Scratching/pinching	☐ Breaking bones
☐ Poking/piercing	☐ Destroying property
☐ Confining/ locking up	☐ Threatening injury/ death
☐ Biting/spitting	☐ Harming pets
☐ Pinning down	☐ Killing pets
☐ Punching	☐ Kidnapping children
☐ Pulling hair	☐ Harming children
☐ Twisting arms	☐ Killing children
☐ Using weapons (stabbing/shooting)	

The Bible warns us against being around those who are violent:

"Do not envy wicked men, do not desire their company; for their hearts plot violence, and their lips talk about making trouble."
(Proverbs 24:1–2)

Sexual Abuse/Violence

Because many men believe that their wives are to be submissive to all of their desires, many women experience *sexual abuse*—some even without realizing it.

Place a check mark (✓) beside any of the following that you have experienced.

▶ **Sexual abuse** includes:

- ☐ *Sexually* degrading attitudes and treatment
- ☐ *Discrimination* based on gender
- ☐ *Withholding* sexual intimacy and romance
- ☐ *Unjust* accusations of extramarital affairs
- ☐ *Brazen* flirtation with members of the opposite sex
- ☐ *Misuse* of Scripture to justify sex "on demand"
- ☐ *Threats* of forced sex
- ☐ *Threats* of going "elsewhere" for sexual gratification
- ☐ *Adultery*
- ☐ *Obscene* gestures
- ☐ *Forced* sex ("mate rape")
- ☐ *Sodomy* (forced oral or anal sex)
- ☐ *Homosexual* acts (rejecting sexual fidelity with wife)
- ☐ *Forced* involvement in perverse sexual acts
- ☐ *Using* objects on sexual parts
- ☐ *Forced* exposure to pornography
- ☐ *Coerced* sexual acts with others

The writer of Hebrews clarifies God's position on the sexual relationship in marriage.

> "Marriage should be honored by all,
> and the marriage bed kept pure,
> for God will judge the adulterer
> and all the sexually immoral."
> (Hebrews 13:4)

Forced Marital Sex

QUESTION: "Is it ever right for a husband to demand sex from or force sex on his wife?"

ANSWER: No. God's purpose for sex in marriage is for procreation and for pleasure.

- Sex within marriage is designed to establish a bond, not a barrier.

- Forced sex is rape.

- Forced sex produces fear that also prevents intimacy.

- Forced sex is lust, not love.

> "Love cares more for others than for self.
> Love doesn't want what it doesn't have.
> Love doesn't ... force itself on others,
> Isn't always 'me first.'"
> (1 Corinthians 13:4–5 MSG)

Neither victimizer nor victim can escape the penetrating gaze of God. The victimizer who has become desensitized to his own violence needs to remember: God is noting every slap, every punch, and every word in an endless string of verbal assaults. Unless there is confession and repentance, a day of accounting and judgment is coming.

The victim who is continually abused by a mate and has become desensitized to the pervasive presence of God needs to remember: Don't ever mistake the silence of God for the absence of God. God has taken note of every abusive incident, and as you pour out your heart to Him, He will always be with you, even during times of suffering.

Never think of God as just a bystander in life, passively watching as the innocent suffer and the wicked prosper. Never! In fact, He became a part of our tragically broken world as the son of the Virgin Mary when God became a man. Jesus even endured unjust suffering at the most pivotal point in history: the Crucifixion. God the Father watched with a broken heart, even though He knew that only His Son's death could pay the penalty for the sins of the world.

When the deepest part of your heart cries His name, He responds with deep love and compassion. God's purpose for allowing you to suffer may seem shrouded in a cloud of mystery. At those times, when you cannot see His hand, you can always trust His heart because *"God is our refuge and strength, an ever-present help in trouble"* (Psalm 46:1).

God's Heart on Violence

▶ **God hates violence.**

"The LORD examines the righteous, but the wicked and those who love violence his soul hates." (Psalm 11:5)

▶ **God judges those who are violent.**

"God said to Noah, 'I am going to put an end to all people, for the earth is filled with violence because of them.'" (Genesis 6:13)

▶ **God is angry with violent behavior.**

"Must they also fill the land with violence and continually provoke me to anger?" (Ezekiel 8:17)

▶ **God prohibits violent people from positions of church leadership.**

"Since an overseer is entrusted with God's work, he must be blameless—not overbearing, not quick-tempered, not given to drunkenness, not violent, not pursuing dishonest gain." (Titus 1:7)

▶ **God commands those who are violent to change.**

"Give up your violence and oppression and do what is just and right." (Ezekiel 45:9)

Anger Toward God

QUESTION: "I am angry at God. If He is just and hates violence, why does He allow abuse?"

ANSWER: You are living with misplaced blame. Realize, God did not create human beings to be puppets to do His will, but rather He gives all people the freedom to choose wrong from right, even those that go against His will. Don't blame God when people choose to do wrong. They are the guilty ones—not God. Rest assured, God is just, and He will punish those who abuse you.

> "God is just: He will pay back trouble
> to those who trouble you."
> (2 Thessalonians 1:6)

God's Heart for the Victim

▶ **God hears the cry of the battered and abused.**

"You hear, O LORD, the desire of the afflicted; you encourage them, and you listen to their cry." (Psalm 10:17)

▶ **God holds the victim of abuse in the palm of His hand.**

"I am the LORD, your God, who takes hold of your right hand and says to you, Do not fear; I will help you." (Isaiah 41:13)

▶ **God sees your pain and hears your cry.**

"'You are the God who sees me,' for she said, 'I have now seen the One who sees me.'" (Genesis 16:13)

▶ **God confirms the victim's value and worth.**

"Are not five sparrows sold for two pennies? Yet not one of them is forgotten by God. Indeed, the very hairs of your head are all numbered. Don't be afraid; you are worth more than many sparrows." (Luke 12:6–7)

▶ **God brings good out of the evil deeds of others.**

"The LORD works out everything for his own ends—even the wicked for a day of disaster." (Proverbs 16:4)

Taking Action against Abuse

QUESTION: **"How do I know whether I should take action when I or someone I know is a victim of abuse?"**

ANSWER: Whenever anyone, yourself included, is being abused, you need always to take some sort of action, even if it does not involve confronting the abuser. A safe rule of thumb is to never confront an abuser in a way or at a place that would put you in harm's way.

- If you know *you are not* being led to confront, then do not feel guilty about not confronting, but you should still report the abuse.

- If you think you are to confront but it is not safe to do so alone, take someone with you who can keep the situation physically and emotionally safe for you. Generally speaking, there is safety in numbers.

- If someone is being abused and the person is powerless to stop the abuse, intervene on the person's behalf. Either confront the abuser yourself, report the abuse to someone who can confront, or direct the victim to someone for counseling and protection.

- If the victim is a minor, the abuse must always be reported to legal authorities where required by law. Even if it is not required by law, it should still be reported.

- If the abused has not directly asked for your help, a good first step is to state simply and kindly that you are available should they ever need to talk or need anything else. This may be all they need to realize that someone cares and that they can find help.

Righteous Job related the role and reputation he had as a rescuer:

**"Whoever heard me spoke well of me,
and those who saw me commended me,
because I rescued the poor
who cried for help, and the fatherless who
had none to assist him."
(Job 29:11–12)**

CHARACTERISTICS

They're all around us, but seldom do you know it, for they are masterful at masking their pain.

Sadly, one out of three women are victims of domestic violence. And these women come from all walks of life—yes, *all*! Whether rich or poor, young or old, whether educated or not, employed or not, religious or not, abuse abides by no boundaries.

It can be your favorite aunt or your friend sitting with you at a little café for lunch, someone you know who perhaps just last night was dragged to the floor and beaten. Those long sleeves she's wearing—year round—could be a hint of horrific abuse at home.

Abused women shroud themselves in secrecy, covering up painful emotions, covering up painful bruises and gashes.

However, God not only sees the abuse, but will also hold the abuser accountable for his degrading, violent behavior.

The Bible says ...

**"Because of your stubbornness
and your unrepentant heart,
you are storing up wrath against yourself
for the day of God's wrath."
(Romans 2:5)**

Like a volcano, abuse doesn't start with a sudden outburst of physical force, but rather with intense, internal pressure that builds to the point of eruption. Abusive patterns develop in three stages that are cyclical and increasingly violent.

Family members who fall victim to the repercussions of these stages feel traumatized by the mere anticipation of a violent outburst. Unfortunately, the escalating nature of abuse is not curbed without intense intervention and appropriate accountability. From the psalmist comes a clear call to action.

> **"Call him [the wicked and evil man]**
> **to account for his wickedness**
> **that would not be found out."**
> **(Psalm 10:15)**

The Cycle of Abuse[10]

▶ **Agitated Stage**

- Anxiety and tension mark the beginning phase of abuse. The abusive man communicates dissatisfaction over something small and blames his mate. Then, by inflicting verbal and emotional abuse, he maintains *passive psychological* control over her, thus creating a fear of some type of pain.

- During this stage, many victims buy into the lies spoken to them and accept responsibility for an abuser's unhappiness. Therefore, they try to adjust their own behavior in an effort to appease him and thereby relieve the tension in their homes. However, these efforts only provoke more anger because the abuser does not want to be appeased, but rather to explode.

"From the fruit of his lips a man enjoys good things, but the unfaithful have a craving for violence." (Proverbs 13:2)

▶ **Acute Stage**

- In this phase, the pressure becomes so intense that the abuser erupts and gives full vent to rage. When violent behavior is unleashed, family members, outsiders, or police are often called on to defuse the rage.

- This acute stage of *aggressive* behavior doesn't last long, but over time these overpowering outbursts become more frequent and more dangerous.

"An angry man stirs up dissension, and a hot-tempered one commits many sins." (Proverbs 29:22).

▶ **Apologetic Stage**

- During this "honeymoon phase," the abuser becomes contrite, even sweet, and the abused feels soothed by these outwardly loving actions. With renewed hope for change and the deep desire to have a successful relationship, the abused views these overtures as genuine, heartfelt apologies and extends forgiveness.

- But, as with all honeymoons, they don't last, and the cycle of anger occurs again ... and again ... and again.

- This temporary honeymoon phase is characterized by the victimizer's dramatic transformation from being villainous to virtuous.

- This transformation is generally demonstrated by some or all of the following behaviors:

  - apologies
  - tears
  - gifts
  - helpfulness
  - promises
  - penitence

  - peacemaking
  - accepting responsibility
  - remorse
  - romance
  - bargaining
  - pleading

However, God says there is a vast difference between remorse and repentance, between regretting past behavior and changing future behavior.

"Godly sorrow brings repentance that leads to salvation and leaves no regret, but worldly sorrow brings death."
(2 Corinthians 7:10)

In an abusive relationship, both partners bring emotional deficits into the relationship, creating an unhealthy dynamic. For the cycle of abuse to be broken, one person in the relationship must change. Either the abuser must stop abusing or the abused must stop accepting abuse.

The abusive man needs to stop perceiving his mate as a piece of property and instead recognize that he is inflicting pain on a precious person created in the image of God—a person highly valued by God. This change of mind-set will make a real difference.

The abused woman needs to place her dependence on God rather than falsely believing she cannot function without her abusive man. A change in mind-set will change an abusive relationship.

It takes only one person to break free from the painful cycle that keeps them both in a downward spiral. Though difficult, release is possible, especially through the power of the Lord.

> **"My eyes are ever on the LORD,**
> **for only he will release**
> **my feet from the snare."**
> **(Psalm 25:15)**

The Setup for Abuse

Notice the relationship between the couple within an abusive relationship:

The Abusive Man	The Abused Woman
Low self-worth	Low self-worth
Emotionally dependent	Emotionally dependent
Emotionally depressed	Emotionally depressed
Feels powerless or impotent	Feels powerless or impotent
Believes in gender supremacy	Believes in family unity
Views her as an unworthy object	Views him as a powerful person
Exaggerated jealousy/ possessiveness	Exaggerated guilt/ shame
Insatiable ego	Insecure ego
Short fuse	Long fuse
Explosive emotions	Stifled emotions
Lives with suspicion	Lives with fear
Fears being betrayed	Fears being abandoned
Afraid of losing her	Afraid of losing financial/emotional security
Uses sex to establish dominance	Uses sex to establish intimacy

The Abusive Man	The Abused Woman
Often abuses alcohol	May or may not abuse alcohol
Displays anger	Denies anger
Blames her for abuse	Accepts blame for abuse
Believes she is the problem	Believes she is the problem
Stressful work environment	Stressful home environment
Possesses weapons	Avoids weapons

The psalmist accurately describes the anguish of the abused:

> **"If an enemy were insulting me, I could endure it; if a foe were raising himself against me, I could hide from him. But it is you ... my companion, my close friend, with whom I once enjoyed sweet fellowship."**
> **(Psalm 55:12–14)**

Changing Abusive Behavior

QUESTION: "Can people ever really change?"

ANSWER: Yes. God would never tell people to change if they couldn't change. However, for people to actually change, they must not only be able to change, but they must desire to change and have a willingness to change.

Jesus' death paid the penalty for our sins. His resurrection broke the power of sin over us. And His Spirit within us provides the power to overcome sinful patterns. Yes, Jesus became a man so that He could die for us, but He also became a man so that He could be an example for us. Changing from the person you are to the person God created you to be involves your mind, will, and emotions with the Holy Spirit providing the power.

"His divine power has given us everything we need for life and godliness through our knowledge of him who called us by his own glory and goodness. Through these he has given us his very great and precious promises, so that through them you may participate in the divine nature and escape the corruption in the world caused by evil desires." (2 Peter 1:3–4)

WHAT IS the Cost of Being Constantly Abused?

There is always a price to be paid for pain, a loss to be suffered by the recipient of abusive words and hurtful acts. The cost is often unseen—an extensive, inner deprivation that can continue to damage the soul for a lifetime. How ironic that the tongue can be both an instrument of healing and an inflictor of heartache.

"The tongue that brings healing is a tree of life, but a deceitful tongue crushes the spirit." (Proverbs 15:4)

The Cost of Being Abused

Loss of ...	Leads to Increased ...
Self-worth	Self-doubt
Self-confidence	Self-consciousness
Self-perception	Self-criticism
Happiness	Emotional flatness
Freedom	Vigilance
Inner peace	"Peace-at-all-costs" mentality
Self-assurance	Anxiety
Security	Insecurity
Trust	Distrust
Sexual identity	Sexual confusion
Clear conscience	Guilt or shame
Friendship	Isolation
Loss of faith	Fear
Safety	Desire to escape
Self-respect	Self-abasement
Optimism	Increased pessimism
Personal pride	Self-hatred
Hope	Despair

Those who suffer the damaging effects of abuse find hope and healing as they cling to the promise of God stated by the apostle Paul.

"Those God foreknew he also predestined to be conformed to the likeness of his Son." (Romans 8:29)

Women in third world countries formerly had few or no options for fleeing an abusive spouse. That scenario is changing considerably with the availability of more residential shelters for battered women and children, as well as nonresidential, temporary shelters. There are also telephone hotlines to aid women in crisis.

Where these options are not available, women should compile a list of "safe homes," a network of people in the community who will provide a haven when they're in harm's way. Some countries also have designated local places of worship as temporary shelters. The Bible encourages us all to *"seek justice, encourage the oppressed"* (Isaiah 1:17).

Staying with an abuser merely to wait for the next violent episode is not your only option. You have more than one viable choice. Safety should be paramount, for until a safe haven is found, you will not have the emotional stability or state of mind to make sound decisions concerning how to get help for your abusive situation and healing for your marriage.

People in abusive relationships adopt various ways of responding to their mates, but you need to know that you have a God who not only watches over you, but who also will guide you in the way you should go if you take refuge in Him. *"You are my hiding place; you will protect me from trouble and surround me with songs of deliverance. I will instruct you and teach you in the way you should go; I will counsel you and watch over you"* (Psalm 32:7–8).

Victims of domestic violence typically choose to respond to their victimizers in one of the following ways.

▶ *The Ostrich Outlook*

The ostrich chooses to deny the situation, minimize its seriousness, or rationalize the abuser's behavior, even to the point of self-blame. "If I just did everything right, my mate wouldn't be this way. It's all my fault!" This choice leads to an even greater loss of self-respect.

▶ *The Martyr Mate*

The martyr decides to be a "silent sufferer" in a destructive relationship. This is a dangerous choice. To survive, this person must sacrifice the voice of truth in order to avoid contradicting the marriage partner and risking a violent reaction.

▶ *The Puppet Partner*

The puppet opts out by disowning personal feelings, denying personal anger, and living emotionally divorced. This choice also leaves the person vulnerable to potential danger. Abusive relationships do not remain static; abuse that goes unchallenged becomes increasingly violent.

▶ *The Merry-Go-Round Mate*

The "merry-go-rounder" has already separated from several abusive partners and is still looking for another partner to provide love and support. With these choices, this person keeps going in circles. Until insight is gained into the reasons for abusive behavior and there is a willingness to take steps to protect self and children, the pattern of abuse will continue. More than likely, this person will find yet another abuser.

▶ *The Boundary Builder*

The boundary builder chooses to set healthy boundaries. Only behavior that is acceptable and nonviolent is tolerated. This positive choice offers the possibility of permanent change. This person prays for God to give the wisdom and courage necessary to stand up to the opposition that will invariably come and also for the ability to follow through with consequences as new standards are established for the way the couple will relate to one another.

▶ *The Departing Dove*

The departing dove leaves—at least for a while—to show the seriousness of the abuse. This choice is an attempt to force the abusive partner to either deal with the abusive behavior or to suffer the consequence of losing a mate. While the abused mate seeks personal counseling, the abusive mate is also encouraged to get professional help. If that help is refused, the couple will remain separated from one another. The departing dove's inner cry is: *"My heart is in anguish within me; the terrors of death assail me. Fear and trembling have beset me; horror has overwhelmed me. I said, 'Oh, that I had the wings of a dove! I would fly away and be at rest—I would flee far away and stay in the desert … I would hurry to my place of shelter, far from the tempest and storm'"* (Psalm 55:4–8).

CAUSES

The way couples relate to each other often mirrors the way their parents related to one another. Most behavioral patterns—both positive and negative—are learned.

In abusive marriages, typically the husband, the wife, or both grew up in an abusive home where conflict resolution skills were not practiced. Therefore, a hostile, abusive environment was "normal" to them.

They didn't realize back then that *their normal* wasn't "normal," and they don't realize now that their normal isn't normal. Sin patterns can be generational, but every succeeding generation has the ability to stop the cycle of abuse that has come down from one generation to the next—with God's help.

The God of the Bible says ...

> **"My people are destroyed
> from lack of knowledge."
> (Hosea 4:6)**

Behavior does not come out of a vacuum, but out of a person's heart, environment, and personal experience. Each person is born with a propensity toward self-will and is raised in an environment that either promotes violence and abuse or promotes love and respect. Beliefs about God, self, and others are formed, and behavior naturally follows.

Research has indicated that young boys who witness violence between their parents triple their chances of becoming abusive husbands. The home where a woman is devalued and traumatized becomes a more impactful model for inciting violence in boys than does being assaulted as a teenager. It is estimated that more than 3 million children are witnesses to spousal abuse in the United States each year as their parents fail to heed the wise words of the writer of Proverbs.[11]

> **"Train a child in the way he should go, and when he is old [mature] he will not turn from it." (Proverbs 22:6)**

▶ **He does it because:**

- He grew up watching abuse between his parents.

- He experienced abuse as a child.

- He views people as possessions rather than persons.

- He "loves things and uses people" instead of loving people and using things.

- He has not been taught how to love.

- He understands love to be "conditional"; if she pleases him, she will avoid his wrath and vindictiveness.

- He thinks he has the right to control her.

- He thinks he has the right to use force on her.

- He fears she will be unfaithful.

- He fears losing her.

- He becomes angry when she shows weakness.

- He sees himself as a victim.

- He thinks she has taken power from him.

- He blames her for his low self-esteem.

- He believes his power demonstrates his superiority.

- He wants to feel significant and in control.

- He possesses an unbiblical view of submission and authority.

- He handles stress immaturely.

- He has few or no coping skills.

- He thinks violence is the way to get even or to retaliate.

- He has learned that violence and other forms of abuse work.

- He hasn't suffered strong enough repercussions to deter him.

The writer of Ecclesiastes explains the impact on an abuser's heart when consequences are delayed. ...

"When the sentence for a crime is not quickly carried out, the hearts of the people are filled with schemes to do wrong." (Ecclesiastes 8:11)

WHY DOESN'T She Leave?

Those who grew up in healthy, non-abusive homes have no frame of reference for those who bow to abuse. But those who grew up in abusive homes know all too well the reasons why the abused not only allow abuse, but also stay with their abusers. They understand the mentality because it is their mentality. They lived it as children, and now they are living it as adults. They are caught in the snare of abuse.

However, the Bible makes it clear ...

"Fear of man will prove to be a snare, but whoever trusts in the Lord is kept safe." (Proverbs 29:25)

An abused woman chooses not to leave her abuser for a variety of reasons—reasons understood by all who have stood in her shoes, walked down her street, and shared in her sorrows. She doesn't leave because of what she firmly believes and falsely feels.

She doesn't leave because of ...[12]

▶ **What she fully believes:**

- She believes she doesn't have a biblical right to separate in order to achieve a healthy relationship.

- She believes abuse is normal and that she must accept it.

- She believes she must protect the family image at all costs.

- She believes family "problems" are private and can't be shared.

- She believes she has to stay because of what spiritual leaders say.

- She believes the promises of her abuser to "never do it again."

- She believes being a peace-at-any-price person is being loyal and godly.

- She believes her husband and children are all she has.

- She believes biblical submission in marriage permits abuse.

- She believes there are no organizations or services to help her.

▶ **What she falsely feels:**

- She feels helpless, as if she has no power to leave or to make it on her own.

- She feels she has no real worth or value.

- She feels manipulated by threats of suicide.

- She feels she deserves to be abused and blames herself.

- She feels isolated from supportive people.

- She feels too much shame to tell about the abuse.

- She feels she is not heard or understood when she does share.

- She feels that others don't want to hear about the abuse.

- She feels that explaining the details of the abuse again costs too much both emotionally and physically.

- She feels that having two parents in an unhealthy relationship is better for the children than having only one healthy parent.

▶ **What she firmly fears:**

- She fears if she "tells" and then he changes, people won't forgive him.

- She fears what her abuser will do if she leaves.

- She fears he will take their children.

- She fears being divorced and/or being a single parent.

- She fears the financial consequences of separation or divorce.

- She fears living all alone.

- She fears being dependent on others for help.

- She fears the "stigma" of others learning about her abuse.

- She fears she is "crazy" because she is continually told that she is crazy.

The abused need to cry out to God ...

> **"Ensure your servant's well-being;**
> **let not the arrogant oppress me."**
> **(Psalm 119:122)**

Separation without Divorce

QUESTION: **"If a wife separates from her husband, is she not ultimately divorcing her husband or at least opening the door to divorce?"**

ANSWER: No, the husband is the one who has opened the door to separation by his violence, not the wife. He is accountable to God for his own sin as well as the consequences of his sin.

▶ Separation is not divorce and does not open the door to divorce, but instead opens the door to safety and obedience to God.

▶ Separation is siding with God regarding His hatred of violence.

"The LORD examines the righteous, but the wicked and those who love violence his soul hates." (Psalm 11:5)

▶ Separation from an abusive husband is trusting God to do what is best for her marriage rather than trusting in anything she might do. She takes literally the Bible's promise to her.

"Trust in the LORD with all your heart and lean not on your own understanding; in all your ways acknowledge him, and he will make your paths straight." (Proverbs 3:5–6)

WHY DOES She Leave?

It is one of the most difficult things she will ever do, and it is one of the best things she could ever do.

Leaving—taking that crucial step to curtail the cycle of abuse—benefits everyone involved and ushers in the opportunity for a fresh new beginning. The woman no longer lives in fear or faces abuse in her own home. The man can better grasp the gravity of the abusive situation and seek biblical counseling. The children are protected and spared further trauma from witnessing their father abuse their mother.

But it is by no means easy for a woman to walk away from the abuser. It is critical to enlist a supportive circle of friends who can help you maintain your resolve and help meet your needs during such a vulnerable time. And above all, seek the guiding, protective hand of God to give you the grace and strength to take that first step out the door.

**"I am he, I am he who will sustain you.
I have made you and I will carry you; I will
sustain you and I will rescue you."
(Isaiah 46:4)**

▶ **She leaves because:**

- She finally realizes that he won't change if circumstances remain the same.

- She understands that leaving may be the only way to motivate him to change.

- She can now see him acting on his threats of severe physical, mental, or emotional abuse.

- She sees his abuse is occurring more frequently.

- She sees he has begun to abuse the children.

- She wants to prevent their children from adopting abusive mind-sets and behaviors.

- She has found help through friends, family, church, or professional organizations.

- She realizes it is not God's will for anyone to be abused.

- She is afraid for her life or for the lives of her children if they stay.

- She realizes there is a thin line between threats and homicide.

She needs to continuously pray ...

**"O righteous God,
who searches minds and hearts,
bring to an end the violence of the wicked
and make the righteous secure."
(Psalm 7:9)**

Scripture reveals that many times godly people did separate physically from their ungodly authorities because submission would have caused them to violate God's standard or His revealed will.

▶ Biblically, we are to submit to our governing "civic" authorities unless doing so would lead to sin or lead to harm. Notice:

- Jesus escaped the murderous plots of the religious leaders.

- The disciples of Jesus defied the mandate from the religious leaders that they stop preaching about Jesus.

- David fled King Saul with God's blessing. Although David was one of the king's subjects, when Saul's actions became violent, David escaped.

**"The Lord was with David but had left Saul. ...
Saul tried to pin him to the wall with his spear,
but David eluded him as
Saul drove the spear into the wall.
That night David made good his escape."
(1 Samuel 18:12; 19:10)**

Submission

QUESTION: "Since the Bible teaches *'submit to one another,'* isn't leaving an abusive relationship against the teaching of the Bible?"

ANSWER: The Bible teaches *mutual* submission in a loving relationship, not *one-way* submission in an abusive relationship. The specific biblical instruction to anyone around a hot-tempered person is separation—get out of harm's way. Even a temporary separation could help bring about a permanent resolution and hopefully eventual reconciliation. A person with out-of-control anger must be willing to stop the abuse and get help. Many times, temporarily removing yourself from a volatile situation will prompt your abuser to seek help for fear of losing you.

The Bible gives this instruction:

"Do not make friends with a hot-tempered man, do not associate with one easily angered."
(Proverbs 22:24)

And the very next verse continues with this warning of staying in a volatile situation:

"Or you may learn his ways and get yourself ensnared."
(Proverbs 22:25)

There is an emotion associated with domestic violence that transcends all geographical boundaries, blinding women from seeing the truth about the abuse they suffer. That emotion is *false guilt*. It beguiles a woman into believing that the bruises, the slashes, the sexual violations really are all her fault, not his.

> *"My guilt has overwhelmed me like a burden too heavy to bear."* (Psalm 38:4)

Blame shifting by the berating man who claims his abusive actions are the result of his mate's missteps can lead to her forming a "false guilt mind-set" if she believes his lies and accepts responsibility for his abusive actions. False guilt adds another unhealthy dynamic to the already wounded emotions of an abused woman.

▶ **She feels guilty because of his accusations that:**

- She disobeyed him.

- She was arguing with him.

- She questioned him about how he was spending money.

- She questioned him about having girlfriends.

- She didn't prepare his meal on time.

- She wasn't sufficiently caring for the home or the children.

- She didn't have his clothes ready for him.

- She refused to have sex with him.

Thus the guilt-ridden, falsely accused woman mentally and emotionally beats herself up, suffering needlessly as she says to herself ...

"My life is consumed by anguish." (Psalm 31:10)

How do the innocent come to bear the guilt of the guilty? Although this seems illogical, it is common among those who are continuously abused. In seeking to understand this painful phenomenon, it is helpful to define some relevant terms.

As the Bible says ...

"Blessed is the man [or woman] who finds wisdom, the man who gains understanding." (Proverbs 3:13)

▶ **Why should she not feel guilty about moving out of harm's way?**

Realize the difference between true guilt and false guilt.

- True guilt is an emotional response as a result of any wrong attitude or action contrary to the perfect will of God—and it refers to the fact of being at fault.

- True guilt is a fact, not a feeling. False guilt is a self-condemning feeling not based on fact.

- False guilt is an emotional response of (1) self-blame even though no wrong has been committed, or (2) self-blame that continues after having committed a sin even though the sin is confessed, repented of, and no longer a part of a person's life.

The prophet Isaiah explains true guilt by saying ...

**"We all, like sheep, have gone astray,
each of us has turned to his own way."
(Isaiah 53:6)**

- False guilt keeps you in bondage to three massive weapons of destruction: shame, fear, and anger.[13]

- False guilt is based on self-condemning feelings that you have not lived up to your own expectations or to the expectations of someone else.

- False guilt is not resolved by confession because there is nothing to confess.

- False guilt is resolved by rejecting lies and believing truth. Revelation 12:10 says that Satan is the *"accuser of our brothers."* He loves to burden believers with false guilt and condemnation. Some of his favorite strategies are: bringing up the past, reminding you of your failures, and making you feel unforgiven and unaccepted by God.

The apostle John describes the aim of Satan and the destiny of Satan:

**"The accuser of our brothers,
who accuses them before our God day and
night, has been hurled down."
(Revelation 12:10)**

Guilt and Shame

QUESTION: "How can I overcome the guilt and shame I feel as a result of being blamed for the abusive things done to me? Did I really deserve this abuse? Was it really my fault?"

ANSWER: Abusers are notorious for blaming their actions on those whom they abuse. Blame shifting is a means of controlling others and breaking down any possibility of resistance.

▶ **Blame shifting** is effective with those ...

- Who have a history of being abused and have been repeatedly told it is their own fault

- Who believe "bad things happen to bad people" so they must be responsible for the abuse

- Who are children, because they are especially vulnerable to false guilt and shame heaped on them by those in authority over them

▶ **But the truth is ...**

- No one deserves abuse.

- No one makes another person sin.

- Abusers alone are responsible for their abusive acts. You are not to blame for what any abuser chooses to do.

▶ **Blame shifters** not only blame their victims but also shame them.

- Shame attacks your "identity." (Guilt says, "I've done something bad," whereas shame says, "I am bad.")

- Shame does not focus on what you've done but on who you are.

- Shame will cause you to feel defective, which, in turn, causes a deep feeling of unworthiness and a continual fear of rejection.

- Shame belongs to the abuser alone—not to you.

Because shame attacks self-worth and produces self-loathing, it must be rooted out and replaced with a biblical view of how God sees you. It must be replaced with the truth.

The psalmist says it this way:

> **"No one whose hope is in you [God]**
> **will ever be put to shame,**
> **but they will be put to shame**
> **who are treacherous without excuse."**
> **(Psalm 25:3)**

ROOT Cause

Some people can't comprehend the *why*'s of abuse. "Why do men do it?" "Why do women accept it?" Within the heart of every person are three God-given inner needs—the needs for love, significance, and security.[14] At times we attempt to meet these needs illegitimately.

Abusers abuse their victims in order to feel significant. Those abused stay in abusive relationships in order to feel secure. Separation feels unbearable, or they feel terrified that the violence will escalate if they leave. God's solution is that both the abused and the abuser look to the Lord to meet their deepest inner needs.

**"The Lord will guide you always;
he will satisfy your needs in a sun-scorched
land and will strengthen your frame.
You will be like a well-watered garden,
like a spring whose waters never fail."
(Isaiah 58:11)**

▶ **WRONG BELIEF:**

The Abuser—Abuses in order to feel significant:

"She is to blame for what's happening. I have the right to expect certain things from my partner, who, after all, belongs to me. If I do not control her, I could lose her, so I'll do whatever it takes to remain in control."

▶ **RIGHT BELIEF:**

The Abuser

"I am the only one responsible for my abusive behavior and the way I respond to people and circumstances. She is not to blame because, no matter what someone else does, I have a choice in how I treat others. Even if I lose her, I'll never lose God. He is my true source of significance and promises to meet my needs."

"My God will meet all your needs according to his glorious riches in Christ Jesus." (Philippians 4:19)

▶ Wrong Belief:

The Abused—Accepts abuse in order to feel secure:

"I'm to blame for what he does to me. I must be doing something wrong. If I just try harder to do what he expects of me, things will get better. If I don't do better, I could lose him along with my security. Or even worse, I could be killed. Pleasing him is my only hope for survival and security."

▶ Right Belief:

The Abused

"I'm not to blame for his abuse, and I have been wrong in thinking my happiness will come from a human relationship. I can choose whether or not I am willing to be around anyone who mistreats me. Even if I lose him, I will never lose Jesus, who lives in me. Because the Lord promises to be my provider, I will depend on Him to meet all of my needs. The Lord is my source of security."

"Your Maker is your husband—the LORD Almighty is his name." (Isaiah 54:5)

Domestic violence does more than damage your body and disturb your thoughts. The pain goes much deeper, breaking your heart. You may feel hopeless and think, *I'll never be able to trust anyone again.* Unfortunately, this kind of heartache cannot simply heal itself over time, and no amount of positive actions can restore your sense of significance or security after being abused by the man you loved and trusted the most. There is only One who can provide eternal security and permanent change of heart.

The Lord offers hope and healing to all who are weary and broken. His path to healing will take time—you will not feel immediate physical safety, but God promises to give His presence, power, and protection to you. If you entrust your heart to Him, He will always walk beside you. You will never again face another day of fear, pain, or torment alone because the Lord says ...

"Be strong and courageous. Do not be afraid or terrified because of them, for the Lord your God goes with you; he will never leave you nor forsake you." (Deuteronomy 31:6)

How to Have Significance and Security That Lasts Forever

#1 God's Purpose for You is *Salvation*.

What was God's motive in sending Christ to earth?

To express His love for you by saving you! The Bible says ...

"God so loved the world that he gave his one and only Son, that whoever believes in him shall not perish but have eternal life. For God did not send his Son into the world to condemn the world, but to save the world through him." (John 3:16–17)

What was Jesus' purpose in coming to earth?

To forgive your sins, to empower you to have victory over sin, and to enable you to live a fulfilled life! Jesus said ...

"I have come that they may have life, and have it to the full." (John 10:10)

#2 Your Problem is *Sin*.

What exactly is sin?

Sin is living independently of God's standard—knowing what is right, but choosing what is wrong. The Bible says ...

"Anyone, then, who knows the good he ought to do and doesn't do it, sins." (James 4:17)

What is the major consequence of sin?

Spiritual "death;" eternal separation from God. Scripture states ...

"Your iniquities [sins] have separated you from your God. ... For the wages of sin is death, but the gift of God is eternal life in Christ Jesus our Lord." (Isaiah 59:2; Romans 6:23)

#3 God's Provision for You is the *Savior*.

Can anything remove the penalty for sin?

Yes! Jesus died on the cross to personally pay the penalty for your sins.

"God demonstrates his own love for us in this: While we were still sinners, Christ died for us." (Romans 5:8)

What can keep you from being separated from God?

Belief in (entrusting your life to) Jesus Christ as the only way to God the Father. Jesus says ...

"I am the way and the truth and the life. No one comes to the Father except through me." (John 14:6)

#4 Your Part is *Surrender*.

Give Christ control of your life—entrusting yourself to Him.

"Jesus said to his disciples, 'If anyone would come after me, he must deny himself and take up his cross [die to your own self-rule] and follow me. For whoever wants to save his life will lose it, but whoever loses his life for me will find it. What good will it be for a man if he gains the whole world, yet forfeits his soul?'" (Matthew 16:24–26)

Place your faith in (rely on) Jesus Christ as your personal Lord and Savior and reject your "good works" as a means of earning God's approval.

"It is by grace you have been saved, through faith—and this not from yourselves, it is the gift of God—not by works, so that no one can boast." (Ephesians 2:8–9)

The moment you choose to receive Jesus as your Lord and Savior—entrusting your life to Him—He comes to live inside you. Then He gives you His power to live the fulfilled life God has planned for you.

If you want to be fully forgiven by God and become the person God created you to be, you can tell Him in a simple, heartfelt prayer like this:

PRAYER OF SALVATION

*"God, I want a real relationship with You.
I admit that many times I've chosen to go
my own way instead of Your way.
Please forgive me for my sins.
Jesus, thank You for dying on the cross
to pay the penalty for my sins.
Come into my life to be
my Lord and my Savior.
Change me from the inside out and make me
the person You created me to be.
In Your holy name I pray. Amen."*

STEPS TO SOLUTION

His arms once sweetly embraced you; they now swing wildly toward you. His arms once tenderly held you; they now severely harm you. You feel devastated, distraught, and devalued.

As a victim of domestic violence you feel submerged in pain both physically and emotionally. You are traumatized and terrorized by a man who fails to heed this command of God: *"Husbands, love your wives, just as Christ loved the church and gave himself up for her"* (Ephesians 5:25). His arms were where you once sought protection; now they terrify you.

But there are other arms—strong arms, opening wide to you, longing to hold you, wanting to convey your worth. To God, you are His precious lamb. He wants to lead you like a shepherd to a place of peace. Turn to Him; ask for His help; seek His wisdom about the scheming wolf in your life. Find refuge and rest in His loving arms. *"He tends his flock like a shepherd: He gathers the lambs in his arms and carries them close to his heart"* (Isaiah 40:11).

KEY VERSE TO MEMORIZE

"Speak up for those who cannot speak for themselves, for the rights of all who are destitute. Speak up and judge fairly; defend the rights of the poor and needy."
(Proverbs 31:8-9)

The woman who sincerely wants to please God but who is not grounded in the Word of God can become captive to an incorrect understanding of "biblical submission." She associates submission with accepting abuse, believing it's her call as a wife to suffer through kicks and punches. But nothing could be further from the heart of God, who never approves a husband's abuse.

One key to correcting the confusion is seeing Scripture in light of its context. Yes, the Bible reads, *"Wives, submit to your husbands"* (Ephesians 5:22), but it also reads, *"Husbands, love your wives, just as Christ loved the church"* (Ephesians 5:25), which is a clear mandate for husbands to treat their wives with compassion and tender care. Here are three helpful steps for examining Scripture accurately and contextually.

▶ Look at the surrounding verses.

▶ Look at the purpose of the passage or book in which the verse is found.

▶ Look at the whole counsel of God's Word on submission and love.

"Do your best to present yourself to God as one approved, a workman who does not need to be ashamed and who correctly handles the word of truth."
(2 Timothy 2:15)

Arguments and Answers

▶ **Argument:** "When Jesus said to 'turn the other cheek,' He meant that you should submit to abuse."[15]

Answer: When you look at these words of Jesus, the context is the issue of rejecting retaliation: Refuse to retaliate evil for evil. Jesus was not advocating submitting to abuse.

"You have heard that it was said, 'Eye for eye, and tooth for tooth.' But I tell you, do not resist an evil person. If someone strikes you on the right cheek, turn to him the other also." (Matthew 5:38–39)

The backdrop of "turning the other cheek" was refusing to take personal revenge rather than promoting or accepting abuse.

▶ **Argument:** "Since Jesus submitted Himself to abuse, if you want to be Christlike, you must also submit to abuse."

Answer: If a person wants to be Christlike, it will be important to notice that on numerous occasions when the enemies of Jesus sought to harm Him, He eluded them and escaped. However, when the time came for Him to take away the sins of the world, Jesus allowed His blood to be the payment price to purchase our forgiveness. Clearly, Jesus did not submit to abuse without purpose.

"Jesus went around in Galilee, purposely staying away from Judea because the Jews there were waiting to take his life. ... Again they tried to seize him, but he escaped their grasp." (John 7:1; 10:39)

▶ **Argument:** "First Peter chapter 2 says we are called to endure *'unjust suffering.'* Therefore, you should take such suffering as 'commendable before God.'"

"It is commendable if a man bears up under the pain of unjust suffering because he is conscious of God." (1 Peter 2:19)

Answer: This passage is not dealing directly with husbands and wives, but specifically speaks to first-century slaves who suffered under the hand of cruel masters. Twisting this passage to condone or justify abuse is a deceptive mishandling of the Word of God. We can learn from this passage that God gives grace to those who endure unjust suffering.

The context of this passage in 1 Peter refers to suffering because you are *"conscious of God,"* which means suffering ridicule, criticism, and rejection because of your faith—not because you are a woman. God does not condone abuse, and abusive men are abusive because of their own ungodliness. In fact, God specifically calls husbands and wives to sacrificially love each other and treat one another *"with respect."*

"Husbands, in the same way be considerate as you live with your wives, and treat them with respect as the weaker partner and as heirs with you of the gracious gift of life, so that nothing will hinder your prayers." (1 Peter 3:7)

▶ **Argument:** "An abused woman should view suffering as her legitimate 'cross to bear.'"

"If anyone would come after me [Jesus], he must deny himself and take up his cross and follow me." (Matthew 16:24)

Answer: Nowhere does the Bible indicate that the cross is an instrument of physical and emotional pain to be inflicted upon a woman by an abusive man. It is not self-centered to escape or stop abuse. In context, Jesus was saying the cross is a symbol of death—death to self-centered living, death to self-rule so that the Lord can rule our hearts and lives. The very next verse confirms that the cross stands for yielding our lives to the Lord, not yielding our lives to abuse.

"Whoever wants to save his life will lose it, but whoever loses his life for me will find it." (Matthew 16:25)

▶ **Argument:** "God made men superior to women."

Answer: God made women and men different from one another, with different roles and functions. The Bible does not say that God regards one gender as superior and the other as inferior, but rather He regards them as equal.

"There is neither Jew nor Greek, slave nor free, male nor female, for you are all one in Christ Jesus." (Galatians 3:28)

▶ **Argument:** "Since Ephesians 5:24 says, '*Wives should submit to their husbands in everything,*' a wife must submit unconditionally, even to abuse."[16]

Answer: This conclusion contradicts other Scripture. A "hierarchy of submission" is demonstrated when the apostles refuse to obey the high priest and instead obey Jesus, who gave them the Great Commission to continue to teach about Him (Matthew 28:19–20). They could have been severely punished by directly disobeying the high priest in order to submit to God.

Similarly, if a husband tells a wife to do something that God says is wrong, she is to disobey her erring husband in order to submit to God.

God clearly states His position that husbands are to treat their wives with respect, as well as His opposition to violence. In all things ...

"We must obey God rather than men!" (Acts 5:29)

▶ **Argument:** "Because the Bible says, *'The husband is the head of the wife,'* a wife must not resist being abused by her husband."

Answer: A wife is to submit to the "headship" (leadership) of her husband, but the Bible nowhere implies she is to submit to the abuse of her husband. She is to respect his position, not be victimized by his power.

In Ephesians 5:23 the husband and wife relationship is compared to the relationship of Christ and the church. Christ is the head of His church, *"his body."* Although the husband is the head of his wife, no head abuses its own body. A husband never chooses to beat his body with a hammer—unless, of course, he is "out of his head" (mentally ill)! Instead, he does whatever he can to protect and provide for his own body. A godly man will treat his wife in the same way.

"The husband is the head of the wife as Christ is the head of the church, his body, of which he is the Savior. ... Husbands ought to love their wives as their own bodies. He who loves his wife loves himself. After all, no one ever hated his own body, but he feeds and cares for it, just as Christ does the church." (Ephesians 5:23, 28–29)

HOW TO Know Whether He Has Really Changed

Habitual patterns of abusive behavior rarely change unless there is significant intervention, professional guidance, or both. Sometimes, however, an abuser becomes so convicted of his harmful ways that the Lord is moved to give the person a new heart, new desires, and the power to change.

If your mate promises that change has occurred, you need wisdom to discern whether the change is only temporary and manipulative or whether your husband is truly taking personal responsibility for his abusive behavior.

"Wisdom will save you from the ways of wicked men, from men whose words are perverse." (Proverbs 2:12)

As you seek to determine the genuineness and reliability of your mate's professed changes ask yourself these questions:

- Do I no longer have a sense of fear when I am with him?

- Has he learned to control his anger without being verbally or emotionally abusive?

- Does he respect my right to disagree?

- Is he able to express feelings of anger in a calm, nonthreatening way?

- Does he communicate feelings other than anger?

- Does he take personal responsibility for inappropriate behavior and no longer blame me or others?

- Do I feel that I am being treated with respect?

- Does he show consistent love and refuse to harbor bitterness toward me?

- Does he include me in decision making?

- Does he ask for my opinions and listen attentively to them?

- Does he share his heart with me?

- Does he express interest in my thoughts, feelings, and desires?

- Does he have an accountability group I can contact?

- Does he respect my need for other relationships?

Scripture is clear about the husband's role:

"Husbands, love your wives and do not be harsh with them." (Colossians 3:19)

If you are experiencing domestic violence, you need to "draw a line in the sand."

Men need to know that their abuse will not be tolerated and that if the line is crossed, a repercussion will follow. Perhaps she will leave the home with the children, or the police will be notified, or their pastor will be called on, or he will be "helped out of the house" by certain men.

Just as important as drawing a line in the sand is this: Ensure that the boundary doesn't get blurred by compromises or by a weak will, with which you cannot enforce the boundary. The only way to prevent abuse in the future is to stop it in the present. What you say you will do—*you must do every time*—or the cycle of abuse will rage on. The following Scripture reflects God's perfect will regarding violence.

> **"No longer will violence be heard in your land." (Isaiah 60:18)**

The following is an acrostic of the word **BOUNDARIES**. As you begin laying a firm foundation for building healthy boundaries ...

Begin a new way of thinking about yourself, about God, and about abuse.

▶ God loves you and created you in His image.

▶ Abuse is a sin against God's creation because God did not create you to be abused.

▶ Don't think that abuse is normal—line up your thinking with God's thinking.

"Do not conform any longer to the pattern of this world, but be transformed by the renewing of your mind. Then you will be able to test and approve what God's will is—his good, pleasing and perfect will." (Romans 12:2)

Overcome fear of the unknown by trusting God with the future.

▶ Personalize and memorize:

"The LORD himself goes before [me] and will be with [me]; he will never leave [me] nor forsake [me]. [I will] not be afraid; [I will] not be discouraged." (Deuteronomy 31:8)

"Do not fear, for I am with you; do not be dismayed, for I am your God. I will strengthen you and help you; I will uphold you with my righteous right hand." (Isaiah 41:10)

"When I am afraid, I will trust in you. ... I sought the LORD, and he answered me; he delivered me from all my fears." (Psalm 56:3; 34:4)

Understand the biblical mandate to hold abusers accountable.

▶ Confrontation is biblical.

▶ Confrontation can be used by God's Spirit to convict the abuser.

▶ Lack of confrontation enables abusers to continue abusing others.

"Call him to account for his wickedness that would not be found out." (Psalm 10:15)

Notify people of your needs (supportive friends, relatives, or others).

▶ They must believe you.

▶ They must be trustworthy.

▶ They must not divulge your new location if you leave.

"Carry each other's burdens, and in this way you will fulfill the law of Christ." (Galatians 6:2)

Develop God's perspective on biblical love, submission, and authority.

▶ Love, submission, and authority never give license for abuse.

▶ Love, submission, and authority are not to be imposed or demanded, but are to be voluntary.

▶ Love, submission, and authority are not designed by God to be a way of life for only some people, but for everyone.

"Submit to one another out of reverence for Christ." (Ephesians 5:21)

Admit your anger and practice forgiveness.

▶ Confirm your hurt.

▶ Confess your anger.

▶ Choose to forgive him, but not necessarily to reconcile with him.

"See to it that no one misses the grace of God and that no bitter root grows up to cause trouble and defile many." (Hebrews 12:15)

Recognize your own codependent patterns of relating and change the way you respond.

▶ Don't respond fearfully, hiding the truth from him.

▶ Don't believe you can change him.

▶ Don't take responsibility for his behavior.

"Am I now trying to win the approval of men, or of God? Or am I trying to please men? If I were still trying to please men, I would not be a servant of Christ." (Galatians 1:10)

Identify healthy boundaries for yourself and commit to maintaining them.

▶ Communicate your boundaries.

▶ State what you will do if he crosses your boundaries.

▶ Follow through when your boundaries are crossed. For example: State firmly, "The next time you use any force against me (or block me from leaving, etc.), I will: call the police, ask you to move out of our home, or I will leave with the children." Then—follow through with the promised action.

"A hot-tempered man must pay the penalty; if you rescue him, you will have to do it again." (Proverbs 19:19)

Ensure your personal safety (and that of your children) immediately.

▶ Have an action plan.

▶ Involve your church. Know ahead of time the person to contact for help.

▶ Know ahead of time where you will go and whom you will call. Have the necessary numbers easily accessible.

"I will lie down and sleep in peace, for you alone, O LORD, make me dwell in safety." (Psalm 4:8)

See your identity as a precious child of God, an identity that cannot change even though your role as a wife may change.

▶ God chose you.

▶ God redeemed you.

▶ God adopted you.

"How great is the love the Father has lavished on us, that we should be called children of God! And that is what we are!" (1 John 3:1)

Setting Boundaries without Risk

QUESTION: "I know that I need to leave my abusive husband and establish boundaries with him. But how do I present the boundaries to him without putting myself at risk?"

ANSWER: All important is *what* you say and *how* you say it (with compassionate strength). At a time when your relationship is stable and peaceful, approach him. If you do not feel safe approaching him alone, ask someone you both respect to be present.

Tell him ...

- "I love you and want our marriage to work."

- "If we could have the best relationship possible, would you want it?"

- "Just as there are penalties for crossing boundary lines in sports, there are penalties for crossing boundary lines in marriage. And you've crossed a boundary line in our *marriage*."

- "I absolutely will not live with an abusive person. Therefore, I have decided to leave and take the children with me."

- "Ultimately, *you will decide* whether we reconcile our marriage."

- "I will know what your decision is by your actions toward me."

- "If you really want us to live together again as husband and wife, I will know by the respect you show me and by the way you treat me."

- "You have the power to make or break our marriage through your actions. *The choice is yours.*"

You must carefully think through and then follow through with the consequences you establish, and thus you will avoid the way of women who are not wise.

**"The wisdom of the prudent
is to give thought to their ways."
(Proverbs 14:8)**

Enlist reinforcements. Battles on the home turf can turn into a full-scale war when an abused woman chooses to leave. It is vital that you surround yourself with an army of people who will support and help protect you. You must also devote the necessary time to make critical preparations (legally, financially, etc.) for independent living. Recognize and understand that threats of harm can escalate when an abuser realizes that his mate is finally going to take decisive action. That is why comprehensive preparation as well as support and help from friends, family, counselors, pastors, and even legal authorities are desperately needed. Never attempt to leave an abuser—by yourself.

Above all, seek refuge in the arms of your Deliverer, asking Him to guide and protect you as you attempt to march away from the war zone. *"Praise be to the Lord my Rock, who trains my hands for war, my fingers for battle. He is my loving God and my fortress, my stronghold and my deliverer, my shield, in whom I take refuge, who subdues peoples under me"* (Psalm 144:1–2).

Violent outbursts can occur at any time. A violent spouse may enter a blind rage when he discovers a different dynamic in the relationship. He begins to fear losing control of you and losing the family. The greatest danger comes when he learns his mate has intentions of leaving. A person who is wise will have prepared for the worst by having a safety plan for leaving. *"A prudent [person] sees danger and takes refuge"* (Proverbs 22:3).

In preparing your strategies for safety:[17]

▶ **Create a list of phone numbers you may need for emergencies.**

- Local Hospital: _____

- Local police: _____

- Women's shelter: _____

- Protection Order Registry: _____

- Attorney: _____

- Work number: _____

- Employer's/supervisor's home number:

  _____

- Church number: _____

- Minister's home number: _____

- Hotline for domestic violence: _____

- Family/Friends: _____

- Other: _____

Pray to God, *"Keep me, O Lord, from the hands of the wicked"* (Psalm 140:4).

▶ **Share the seriousness of your situation with trustworthy people.**

- Ask whether you could stay with them at a moment's notice if the need arises.

- Ask neighbors to call the police if they hear screams or hitting.

- Select a code word (such as "blue eggs") or a signal (turning on a certain light) to use as a sign for your neighborhood friends and family to call the police.

- Store a bag of extra clothing and money at a confidant's house.

- Talk with a doctor and/or nurse about the violence. (Ask them to take photographs of your injuries and to document the abuse in your medical records.)

- Contact a local shelter to discuss your options and ask them to help you make a safety plan.

Pray to God, *"Blessed is he who has regard for the weak; the Lord delivers him in times of trouble"* (Psalm 41:1).

▶ **Plan an escape route.**

- Identify which emergency exits you can use (doors, windows, elevator, stairwell) and practice getting out safely.

- If an argument begins, move away from any room containing weapons (such as the kitchen).

- Move to a room that has an exit (not a bathroom, a closet, or a small space where the abuser could trap you).

- Rehearse your escape plan with your children.

"Make level paths for your feet and take only ways that are firm." (Proverbs 4:26)

▶ **Teach your children "safety secrets."**

- Teach them to not get into the middle of a fight, even if they want to help you.

- Teach them to stay out of the kitchen (away from knives).

- Teach them how to give your address and phone number to trusted and known adults.

- Teach them how to call the police.

- Teach them whom to call for help.

- Teach them how to quickly and quietly escape (through a back door or window).

- Teach them when to escape (such as when violence erupts or when they feel threatened).

- Teach them where to go for safety.

"Through knowledge the righteous escape." (Proverbs 11:9)

▶ **Place physical evidence of violence with a trusted confidant or in a safety deposit box.**

- Documentation of physical injuries to you and your children

- Pictures of damaged property (such as broken furniture, doors, and walls)

- A log of the abuse by date and event

- Physical evidence of his threats from letters, e-mails, voice mail, text messages, and answering machine messages

"They do not realize that I remember all their evil deeds. Their sins engulf them; they are always before me." (Hosea 7:2)

▶ **Identify essential or meaningful items you can gather quickly (but remember safety must be your first concern).**

- Address book

- Children's favorite toys and blankets

- Medicines

- Pictures

- Sentimental items

- Your personal pets

"Gather up your belongings to leave the land, you who live under siege." (Jeremiah 10:17)

▶ **Keep important papers and documents easily accessible and together in one place (but remember everything on this list can be replaced).**

- Bank books, money, credit cards

- Birth certificates

- Current unpaid bills

- Deeds and other legal records (lease/rental agreement, house deed, mortgage payment book)

- Divorce papers

- Driver's license and registration

- Family medical records

- Insurance papers (health, car, house)

- Passport, green card, visa, work permit

- Protective order/restraining order (keep with you at all times)

- School records (K–12)

- College diploma

- Social security cards

- Welfare identification

- Résumé

- Transcripts of children in college

- SAT/ACT scores

"Wisdom reposes in the heart of the discerning." (Proverbs 14:33)

▶ **Cover your bases before leaving.**

- Accumulate some emergency cash and keep it hidden or give it to a confidant for safekeeping.

- Transfer important digital files to external media and then delete them from the computer.

- Hide an extra set of car keys (also house and office keys).

- Open a checking and/or savings account in your name.

- Cancel any shared bank accounts or credit cards.

- Change passwords to online accounts that you'll need to access.

- Open a post office box in your name.

- Put aside jewelry, silver, or other valuables that he would not miss and that could be quickly sold for cash.

"If you are wise, your wisdom will reward you." (Proverbs 9:12)

HOW TO Protect Yourself Outside the Home

Even if an abused woman no longer lives under the same roof with her abuser, she may not be out of harm's way. Finding opportunities to inflict harm become more challenging for abusers, but some are relentless in their pursuit for revenge.

Safety can be a constant challenge for you whether alone or in a crowd, at home, at work, in a subway, or in a car. There is comfort to be found behind locked doors and bolted windows, but those aren't available in public places. So how do you live without fear and a sense of constant vulnerability?

Thankfully, safety steps can help reduce the risk of further abuse, but never fail to remember that the Lord God Almighty, not your abusive husband, is sovereign over your life. Seek refuge in Him.

"The name of the Lord is a strong tower; the righteous run to it and are safe." (Proverbs 18:10)

▶ **Safety steps for being out and about**

- Change your regular travel habits.

- Try to get rides with different people.

- Shop and bank in a different place.

- Keep your court order and emergency numbers with you at all times.

- Obtain a cell phone and program it to call an emergency number or the police. (Keep it with you at all times.)

"The Lord will keep you from all harm—he will watch over your life." (Psalm 121:7)

▶ **Safety steps for being at work**

- Confide in a coworker about your unsafe situation.

- Explain your situation to the head of security at the office building.

- Give a picture of your abuser to security, your supervisor, and friends at work.

- Ask your supervisors if they can make it harder for your abuser to find you at work.

- Keep a copy at work of your court order, if you have one.

- Ask someone to screen your calls, if possible.

- Save abusive and threatening voice mails and e-mails.

- Don't go to lunch alone.

- Ask a security guard, friend, or coworker to walk you to and from your car, bus, or other mode of transportation.

- Ask if your employer can help you find community resources.

"Rescue the weak and needy; deliver them from the hand of the wicked." (Psalm 82:4)

HOW TO Use the Law in the United States

Sadly, many abused women are so beaten down that they feel powerless to do anything to free themselves from the bondage they mistakenly believe is unbreakable. In truth, it is not only their abusers who keep them in bondage but also their own passivity, rooted in fear and insecurities. They choose to stay in abusive relationships rather than definitively act to bring about an end to their violent home life.

But today, unlike them, you can choose differently. Through the legal system and other strong community support networks, you can begin developing a plan to break the cycle of abuse once and for all. Do not believe the lies that you have to stay and endure abuse or that no one can or wants to help you. Help is available from those around you and from the One above you.

"Rulers hold no terror for those who do right, but for those who do wrong. ... Do what is right and he will commend you. For he is God's servant to do you good. But if you do wrong, be afraid, for he does not bear the sword for nothing. He is God's servant, an agent of wrath to bring punishment on the wrongdoer." (Romans 13:3–4)

Take Action!

▶ **If you stay in your home and obtain a restraining order/protective order:**

- Inform family members, friends, neighbors, and coworkers of the court order.

- Ask them to be ready to call the police if your abuser appears and refuses to leave.

- Get an unlisted phone number.

- Take a good self-defense course.

- Keep a phone in a room you can lock from the inside.

- When you need to call the police, do so quickly.

- If police officers come, tell them what happened and get their names and badge numbers.

To those in law enforcement, the Bible says ...

"Let the fear of the LORD be upon you. Judge carefully, for with the LORD our God there is no injustice or partiality or bribery." (2 Chronicles 19:7)

▶ **If your home is not safe and secured:**

- Install new locks on outside doors.

- Install deadbolt locks.

- Install locks on the windows and on the inside of your bedroom door.

- Install a security system.

- Install smoke detectors.

- Install an outside lighting system.

"You will know that your home is safe."
(Job 5:24 NLT)

▶ **Protect your children and yourself by allowing the judge to issue protective orders that:**

- Order your abuser to stay away from you and your children.

- Order him to leave your home.

- Order you to take temporary custody of your children and ordering him to pay you temporary child support.

- Order the police to come to your home while he picks up personal belongings.

- Order you to take possession of the car, furniture, and other belongings.

- Order him to go to a batterers' intervention program.

- Order him to not call you at work.

- Order him to turn over his guns to the police.

"We know that the law is good if one uses it properly." (1 Timothy 1:8)

▶ **If you are receiving harassing phone calls:**

- Consider caller ID/tracking.

- Consider rejecting anonymous calls.

- Consider call screening.

- Consider call blocking.

- Consider call tracing.

- Consider call waiting/caller ID.

- Consider do not disturb (a function on some phones).

- Consider priority ringing.

"This is what the Lord Almighty says: 'Give careful thought to your ways'." (Haggai 1:5)

▶ **If you are worried about your safety or the safety of your children during scheduled visits:**

- Show the judge pictures of your injuries.

- Tell the judge that you do not feel safe when your abuser comes to your home to pick up the children to visit with them.

- Ask the judge to order him to pick up and return the children at the police station or some other safe place.

- Ask that visits be only at very specific times so the police will know by reading the court order whether he is there at the wrong time.

- Tell the judge if your abuser has harmed or threatened the children; ask that visits be supervised; think about who could do that for you.

- Get a certified copy of the court order.

"Protect me from men of violence who plan to trip my feet." (Psalm 140:4)

▶ **If you are concerned about your safety during any criminal or courthouse proceedings:**

- Show the prosecutor your court orders.

- Show the prosecutor medical records containing your injuries or pictures, if you have them.

- Tell the prosecutor the name of anyone who is helping you (a victim advocate or a lawyer).

- Tell the prosecutor about any witnesses to your injuries or abuse.

- Ask the prosecutor to notify you ahead of time if your abuser is getting out of jail.

- Sit as far away from your abuser as you can; you don't have to look at or talk to him; you don't have to talk to his family or friends if they are there.

- Bring a friend or relative with you to wait until your case is heard.

- Tell a bailiff or sheriff that you are afraid of your abuser, and ask them to look out for you.

- Make sure you have your court order before you leave.

- Ask the judge or the sheriff to retain him for a while when court is over so that you can leave quickly without having any unwanted interaction.

- Call the police immediately if you think he is following you when you leave.

- Take your protection order with you if you have to travel to another state, either for work or for safety. It is valid everywhere.

"This is what the LORD says: 'Stand at the crossroads and look; ask for the ancient paths, ask where the good way is, and walk in it, and you will find rest for your souls.'" (Jeremiah 6:16)

"You will go on your way in safety, and your foot will not stumble." (Proverbs 3:23)

**"The LORD is my rock, my fortress and my deliverer; my God is my rock, in whom I take refuge. He is my shield and the horn of my salvation, my stronghold."
(Psalm 18:2)**

The United States Bill of Rights, the first ten amendments to the U.S. Constitution, stands as a fundamental symbol for individual freedoms. Among other constraints, Congress can pass no law that prohibits the free exercise of religion, nor can it deprive any person of life, liberty, or property without due process of law.

And so it goes within the marriage relationship. Know the rights you have that are firmly embedded in an even more trustworthy document—*the Bible, the Word of God*. Rights to operate by faith, not by fear; rights to seek to live a holy life, not a hellish one marked by abuse.

> **"God did not call us to be impure,**
> **but to live a holy life."**
> **(1 Thessalonians 4:7)**

Some people claim that when you come into a relationship with Christ, you give up all of your rights. This simply is not true. You always have the God-given right to live your life according to God's Word in order to accomplish God's will. For example, if your marriage partner tries to pressure you to commit a sinful act by using Scripture out of context (perverting the purpose of *"Wives, submit to your husbands"*), God's will is that you *not* do it. Instead, you *"must obey God rather than men!"* (Acts 5:29).

Biblical Bill of Rights

Within the marriage relationship ...

#1 God's will is that you treat one another with respect.

"The wife must respect her husband."
(Ephesians 5:33)

"Husbands, in the same way be considerate as you live with your wives, and treat them with respect."
(1 Peter 3:7)

#2 God's will is that you experience mutual submission.

"Submit to one another out of reverence for Christ." (Ephesians 5:21)

#3 God's will is that you speak truth and have truth spoken to you in a loving manner.

"Speaking the truth in love, we will in all things grow up into him who is the Head, that is, Christ." (Ephesians 4:15)

#4 God's will is that you express anger and have anger expressed toward you in appropriate ways.

"'In your anger do not sin': Do not let the sun go down while you are still angry." (Ephesians 4:26)

#5 God's will is that you both spend personal time alone.

"Very early in the morning, while it was still dark, Jesus got up, left the house and went off to a solitary place, where he prayed." (Mark 1:35)

#6 God's will is that you use your unique talents and gifts to serve others.

"Each one should use whatever gift he has received to serve others, faithfully administering God's grace in its various forms." (1 Peter 4:10)

#7 God's will is that you enjoy freedom from fear.

"You did not receive a spirit that makes you a slave again to fear, but you received the Spirit of sonship. And by him we cry, 'Abba, Father.'" (Romans 8:15)

#8 God's will is that you both seek emotional and spiritual support from others.

"Let us not give up meeting together ... but let us encourage one another." (Hebrews 10:25)

#9 God's will is that you report abuse to governmental authorities.

"Submit yourselves for the Lord's sake to every authority instituted among men ... who are sent by him to punish those who do wrong and to commend those who do right. ... The authorities that exist have been established by God. Consequently, he who rebels against the authority is rebelling against what God has instituted, and those who do so will bring judgment on themselves." (1 Peter 2:13–14; Romans 13:1–2)

#10 God's will is that you leave an abusive relationship, when necessary.

"The prudent see danger and take refuge, but the simple keep going and suffer for it." (Prov. 27:12)

Is a husband's "headship" a license for wife abuse? To the contrary! Does your head seek to hurt your hand? Does your brain tell you to break your bone? No, your head protects and provides for your body at all costs. Likewise, the husband, as the God-ordained head of the wife, is to protect her from harm, or else he forfeits his right to headship. How significant that Christ, as the Head of the church, not only loved her, but gave Himself up for her!

—June Hunt

THE UNITED NATIONS UNIVERSAL DECLARATION OF HUMAN RIGHTS

Articles I, III, and V, 1948
"All human beings are born free and equal in dignity and rights. ... Everyone has the right to life, liberty and security of person. ... No one shall be subjected to torture or to cruel, inhuman or degrading treatment or punishment."

SCRIPTURES TO MEMORIZE

What is the attitude of **the Lord** toward **those who love violence**?

*"The LORD examines the righteous, but the wicked and **those who love violence** his soul hates."* (Psalm 11:5)

Is it wrong to report a **hot-tempered man** who may have to **pay** a **penalty**?

*"A **hot-tempered man** must **pay** the **penalty**; if you rescue him, you will have to do it again."* (Proverbs 19:19)

If I feel I'm in **danger**, should I **take refuge**?

*"The prudent see **danger** and **take refuge**, but the simple keep going and suffer for it."* (Proverbs 27:12)

What should I do about someone in my life who is **hot-tempered** and **easily angered**?

*"Do not make friends with a **hot-tempered man**, do not associate with one **easily angered**."* (Proverbs 22:24)

Who can you trust if you can't trust **your** own **husband**?

*"Your Maker is **your husband**—the LORD Almighty is his name."* (Isaiah 54:5)

NOTES

1. *What Every Congregation Needs to Know About Domestic Violence*, (Seattle, WA: Center for the Prevention of Sexual and Domestic Violence, 1994), n.p.

2. Carol Forsloff, "Health Workers Facilitate Wife Beating," *Digital Journal*, Feb. 1, 2009, http://www.digitaljournal.com/article/266301.

3. *American Heritage Electronic Dictionary* (Houghton Mifflin, 1992).

4. *American Heritage Electronic Dictionary.*

5. James Strong, *Strong's Hebrew Lexicon*, electronic ed., Online Bible Millennium Ed. v. 1.13 (Timnathserah Inc., July 6, 2002).

6. Francis Brown, Samuel Rolles Driver, Charles Augustus Briggs, *Enhanced Brown-Driver-Briggs Hebrew and English Lexicon*, electronic ed. (Oak Harbor, WA: Logos Research Systems, 2000), 329.

7. Kathy L. Cawthon, *Getting Out: An Escape Manual for Abused Women* (Lafayette, LA: Huntington House, 1996), 22–23; *Family Violence and Addiction: Implications for Treatment* (n.p.: Texas Department of Human Services, 1989).

8. *What Every Congregation Needs to Know About Domestic Violence*, n.p.

9. Cawthon, *Getting Out*, 89–92.

10. Patricia Riddle Gaddis, *Battered But Not Broken: Help for Abused Wives and Their Church Families* (Valley Forge, PA: Judson, 1996), 27–29; Kay Marshall Strom, *In the Name of Submission: A Painful Look at Wife Battering* (Portland, OR:

Multnomah, 1986), 44–46; Lenore E. Walker, *The Battered Woman* (New York: HarperPerennial, 1979), 55–70.

11. Donald G. Dutton, "Witnessing Parental Violence as a Traumatic Experience Shaping the Abusive Personality" in Robert A. Geffner, Peter G. Jaffe, Marlies Sudermann, editors, *Children Exposed to Domestic Violence: Current Issues in Research, Intervention, Prevention, and Policy Development* (New York: The Haworth Maltreatment & Trauma Press, 2000), 61.

12. McDill and McDill, *Shattered and Broken*, 76–82; Ginny NiCarthy and Sue Davidson, *You Can Be Free: An Easy-to-Read Handbook for Abused Women* (Seattle, Wash.: Seal, 1989), 16–19; Strom, *In the Name of Submission*, 35–39.

13. Brent Curtis, *Guilt*, Institute for Biblical Counseling Discussion Guide, ed. Tom Varney (Colorado Springs, CO: NavPress, 1992), 14–29.

14. Lawrence J. Crabb, Jr., *Understanding People: Deep Longings for Relationship*, Ministry Resources Library (Grand Rapids: Zondervan, 1987), 15–16; Robert S. McGee, *The Search for Significance*, 2nd ed. (Houston, TX: Rapha, 1990), 27–30.

15. Marie M. Fortune, *Keeping the Faith: Questions and Answers for the Abused Woman*, (San Francisco: HarperSanFrancisco, 1987), 28–29.

16. Strom, *In the Name of Submission*, 56–57.

17. *Peace At Home, Domestic Violence: The Facts*, (Somerville, MA: Peace at Home, 2004), 14–15, http://www.betterman.org/dv-the-facts.pdf.

HOPE FOR THE HEART TITLES

Adultery ....ISBN 9781596366848
Alcohol & Drug Abuse ....ISBN 9781596366596
Anger ....ISBN 9781596366411
Anorexia & Bulimia ....ISBN 9781596369313
Bullying ....ISBN 9781596369269
Chronic Illness & Disability.............................ISBN 9781628621464
Codependency ....ISBN 9781596366510
Conflict Resolution ....ISBN 9781596366473
Confrontation ....ISBN 9781596366886
Considering Marriage ....ISBN 9781596366763
Critical Spirit ....ISBN 9781628621310
Decision Making ....ISBN 9781596366534
Depression ....ISBN 9781596366497
Domestic Violence..ISBN 9781596366824
Dysfunctional Family ....ISBN 9781596369368
Fear ....ISBN 9781596366701
Financial Freedom ....ISBN 9781596369412
Forgiveness...ISBN 9781596366435
Friendship ....ISBN 9781596368828
Gambling ....ISBN 9781596366862
Grief ....ISBN 9781596366572
Guilt ....ISBN 9781596366961
Hope ....ISBN 9781596366558
Loneliness ....ISBN 9781596366909
Manipulation..ISBN 9781596366749
Marriage...ISBN 9781596368941
Overeating...ISBN 9781596369467
Parenting ....ISBN 9781596366725
Perfectionism...ISBN 9781596369214
Procrastination ....ISBN 9781628621648
Reconciliation..ISBN 9781596368897
Rejection ....ISBN 9781596366787
Self-Worth...ISBN 9781596366688
Sexual Integrity ....ISBN 9781596366947
Singleness ....ISBN 9781596368774
Spiritual Abuse ....ISBN 9781628621266
Stress ....ISBN 9781596368996
Success Through Failure ....ISBN 9781596366923
Suicide Prevention..ISBN 9781596366800
Trials ....ISBN 9781628621891
Verbal & Emotional Abuse ....ISBN 9781596366459
Victimization...ISBN 9781628621365

www.aspirepress.com